Awaken Your Author Mindset

Finish Writing Your Book Fast

Author Success Foundations, Book 1

by

Christopher di Armani

Copyright © 2018 Christopher di Armani

All rights reserved.

ISBN-13: 978-1988938059

Editor: Nicolas Johnson

Published By:
Botanie Valley Productions Inc.
PO Box 507
Lytton, BC V0K 1Z0
http://BotanieValleyProductions.com

Dedication

This book is dedicated to my sweet and loving wife Lynda. Without her unwavering support none of this would be possible.

Acknowledgments

Without the assistance of my editor, Nicolas Johnson, I can't imagine how this book would read. He tears my words apart from every conceivable angle, then offers thoughtful and constructive criticism on how best to fix the destruction at our feet.

I thank God for Nicolas Johnson and his talents, daily.

#EditorsMatter

I also wish to express my heartfelt gratitude to the following individuals who took time from their own busy lives to critique this manuscript. Their willingness to assist a total stranger humbles me.

Kim Steadman (KimSteadman.com)
Sharilee Swaity (Facebook.com/Sharilee.Swaity)

Table of Contents

Imagine The Possibilities! — 7

Yes, You Can Write A Book — 9
- What We Believe We Will Achieve — 9
- We Focus On What We Value — 11
- Inspiration is for Amateurs — 13
- The Mathematics of Writing a Book — 14
- Practice Makes Perfect — 16
- Personal Responsibility Will Change Your Life — 17
- Make a Decision... Follow it with Action — 18

Define and Set Your Goals — 21
- What is a Goal? — 21
- Failure Is Not An Option — 24

Self-Honesty: Your Starting Point — 27
- Honesty is the Best Medicine — 27
- Determine Your Current Writing Speed — 28
- Writing Prompts — 29

Resistance to Change in Yourself and Others — 31
- Change is Required — 31
- The Seven Commandments of the Writing Life — 33
- The Distance Between Should and Do — 34
- Success is Terrifying — 34
- Change is Scary — 35
- Fears to Overcome — 37
- The Nike Challenge — 37

Three Steps to Prolific Writing (Plus Two Suggestions) — 39

Make a Decision	39
Make a Commitment	40
Take Action	40
Deadlines are for Professionals	40
Be Dedicated	41
You Do Not Accomplish What You Do Not Schedule	43
Scheduling 101	43
Conclusion: The 7 Steps to Building a Fruitful Writing Life	45
Download the Free Workbook	48
The Plan for Success is Written on Paper	48
The Road to Success Begins With Your Morning Routine	49
One Last Thing!	50
About Christopher di Armani	52
Books by Christopher di Armani	
The Simple 3-Step Secret to Slaughter Writer's Block And Vanquish it Forever	54
TOP SECRET - Inspiration, Motivation and Encouragement 701 Essential Quotes for Writers	55
Justin Trudeau - 47 Character-Revealing Quotes from Canada's 23rd Prime Minister and What They Mean for You	56
From Refugee to Cabinet Minister: Maryam Monsef's Meteoric Rise to Power and her Spectacular Fall From Grace	57
Filming Police is Legal - How to Hold Police Accountable While Staying Out of Jail	58
Appendix - Free Writing Resources	59
Endnotes	61

Imagine The Possibilities

You want to write a book.

You *need* to write a book. It's in your DNA, yet for reasons you cannot comprehend, you just can't finish the job.

Your dream of a published book, now tarnished and neglected, rots in some dark corner of your mind. Your tears of frustration, like cold October rain, further the decay of your already broken will. Feelings of failure and self-doubt leave you bereft and hopeless. Your unfinished manuscript rusts away like a broken-down vehicle abandoned on the side of Publication Highway.

If this describes your situation today, fantastic. Yes, *fantastic*. You admitted you don't know the answers. All your frustration, shame and self-loathing for your failure to finish your book forced you to admit, finally, you need help. The first step to solve a problem is to admit a problem exists. Nothing changes, nothing can change without this admission.

Then you took a second step. You asked for help. Sure, you didn't say the words out loud, but you asked for help nonetheless.

You picked up this book.

Together, we will clean out the rot of despair and restore your desire to write. We will grind the rust off the neglected hull of your manuscript. We will buff your motivation and self-discipline until they shine like the sun glistening off freshly-polished paint.

We will fill your gas tank and learn how to keep it topped up every day. We will throw away those flat, decaying tires, and replace them with shiny new white-walls. We will learn how to keep those tires inflated, regardless of the terrain ahead.

Then we will charge the dead battery of your self-discipline, jump-start your author engine and roar down Publication Highway until your dream, a published book, becomes reality.

A word of caution before we begin. This is not your normal writing book. In fact, it contains very little advice on how to write. Instead, I focus on creating the foundation, the author mindset, required to finish your book.

With this foundation in place, you will fulfill your dreams. Yes, including your dream of a published book.

Want to write your book this year? You can.

Want to write your book in 6 months? You can.

Want to write your book in 30 days or less? You can.

Any of these possibilities, no matter how outlandish they may appear, are open to you when you follow this simple, three-step process.

Step 1 – Make a Decision.

Step 2 – Commit 100% to your decision.

Step 3 – Follow your decision with the Action required.

This book teaches you how to develop your bullet-proof Author Mindset, to create a system guaranteed to deliver success, to build the daily habits required to work this system every single day.

The road from where you are right now to your new reality is simple. I said *simple*, not easy. Commitment is hard. Action is even harder. But the results are… incredible.

The choice is yours. If you continue to do what you've always done… you'll just get what you already have - an unfinished manuscript, more disappointment, discarded dreams and self-loathing than you can handle.

You will *never* finish your book.

Now, imagine the possible. Imagine you wake up each morning filled with the satisfied glow of accomplishment with yesterday's word count and the knowledge you will write more today. Imagine you open a package and discover it is filled with copies of your book. Watch the movie in your mind as you pick up one of the books and hold it in your hands. Feel the cover under your fingertips. Does your heart pound when you look upon your name printed in big, bold letters? Does a sense of pride in achievement well up inside you?

Of course, it does.

Join me. Allow me to be your guide, to help you construct a mindset, a solid foundation for your finished manuscript and published becomes, not just possible, but inevitable.

This is the power of the Author Mindset.

Chapter 1

Yes, You Can Write A Book

What We Believe We Will Achieve

There is a difference between wishing for a thing and being ready to receive it. No one is ready for a thing until he believes he can acquire it. The state of mind must be belief, not mere hope or wish. Open-mindedness is essential for belief. Closed minds do not inspire faith, courage, and belief.[1]

— Napoleon Hill

The human mind is a miraculous device. It believes everything you tell it.

Everything.

Belief creates reality. Your power to believe is a practical tool to manifest a reality beyond your wildest imaginations. How is this possible? It's how the mind operates. Your mind is a super-computer, the most powerful in existence. It can create any reality you choose.

Do you believe life is hard? If so, your belief is reflected in your day-to-day experience and sure enough, your life is difficult.

Do you believe writing a book is hard? Then writing is hard, guaranteed.

To use an old computer programming analogy:

Garbage In, Garbage Out.

When you put crap into your mind, you get crap right back out. When you fill your mind with positive thoughts and ideas, you get great results out.

Try this simple test. Think back to the worst day of your life. Remember the most tragic moment of that day and focus on it for ten seconds. Your mind drinks in the full power of the event and reflects it back into your body and your emotions.

Do tears well up in your eyes? Does your heart break anew? Is the pain of that day as fresh in this moment as it was at the time?

Incredible, right?

Take two or three deep breaths to release this energy from your mind and return to the present moment.

Now, I want you to remember the happiest moment of your life. Focus on this positive memory for ten seconds. Do you feel it? Does your face break into a smile? Does your heart sing with joy as you relive the same emotions you experienced then?

Of course. Your entire being is uplifted. Your emotions soar to the heavens, all because of a single thought. Ten short seconds and your entire emotional outlook changed.

With all this raw power, imagine your accomplishments when you focus on a single goal for 60 minutes per day, six days per week for the next twelve months.

Our minds act, not upon reality as it is, but as we *perceive* it.

What we believe, we achieve.

The power of our mind to believe is also its greatest curse. When we examine our beliefs in the deepest, darkest recesses of our minds, we are shocked and horrified at the garbage dump we left to rot down there. This trash-filled wasteland exists in our minds - nowhere else - and we put it there. Worse, we haul it out each morning and dump its putrid waste all over our tomorrows without a single, conscious thought.

Do you believe writing a book is hard? Then writing every day is excruciating. However, if you believe as I do, writing 5,000 words per day is easy, then it is easy.

See how it works? Our beliefs create our reality. Success, in any endeavor, requires we rewire our minds to believe a new thought - a positive thought - designed to push us straight to our goals. The negative garbage we believe today drags us down like a boat anchor.

Don't get me wrong. I did not churn out 5,000 words per day overnight. I worked at it. I built my stamina, skills and determination every single day for years. It took time, energy and commitment to write every day and rewire my belief system. I removed the word "impossible" from my thoughts.

I want to shortcut your journey down Publication Highway. Sure, you must still do the work, but once you believe 5,000 words per day is possible for you, nothing can prevent you from achieving it. Nothing.

I didn't believe I could do it either, at first. I challenged myself to write something, *anything*, every single day. I sometimes wrote as much as 300 words a day, mostly less, but I wrote every day. Over time my word count grew, until I broke 500 words a day. Then 1,000, then 1,500, then 2,000 words per day.

Once I broke the 2,000 word barrier, my daily word count doubled again, almost overnight. Now, 5,000 words a day isn't much of a challenge at all.

Why? My past experience and success "proved" to me it was possible.

During National Novel Writing Month 2017 (NaNoWriMo), I wrote the entire first draft of a fiction novel, over 106,000 words, in 29 days. I only wrote 21 of those 29 days, too. Family and work filled the other eight. I also wrote over 20,000 words in just three days in the final week and - here's the kicker - I felt I didn't work hard at all.

I believed it was possible, and that's the key.

Hey, just because I write 5,000 words per day, there's no reason you can't blow me out of the water and write 6,000, 8,000, or even 10,000 words a day.

I bet you can. I bet you will.

"And whatever things you ask in prayer, believing, you will receive."
— Matthew 21:22 (*The Bible – New King James Version*)

We Focus On What We Value

What do you focus on most often? What's your life's obsession? Whatever it is, it will shape, mold, and direct your life.[2]
— Anthony Robbins

What we focus our attention upon is what we value. Do you want to know what you value most? Answer the question, "Where do I spend my time?"

Our answer reveals a disturbing truth. Our actions contradict our best intentions. We value the wrong things.

Do you value writing? Do your actions reflect your belief?

The honest answer to the question "Where do I spend my time?" is pretty horrifying. Facebook, Twitter, Pinterest, television… and a ton of similar items probably top your list.

Here's another thought, just in case the first question didn't depress you enough. Do you struggle to "find time to write" or do you consciously "make time to write"? Another scary answer, right?

Here's a simple cure.

FOCUS.

Follow.

One.

Course.

Until.

Successful.

When you focus on one goal to the exclusion of all else, you make incredible progress. Writers all over the world love NaNoWriMo for this reason. No matter where they live or what language they speak, hundreds of thousands of writers commit to the same goal each November: 50,000 words in 30 days. Others modify the goal to suit their needs, as I did this year. Instead of a word count, I committed to write the first draft of my latest fiction novel in 30 days.

Challenging? Absolutely.

Difficult? It felt hard at times, sure, but because I was determined to achieve my goal, the words came easily most of the time.

The trick is to carry the NaNoWriMo commitment, dedication and focus over to the other eleven months of the year. It's far easier than you think, but first we must address another destructive myth: Inspiration.

> *No one can serve two masters; for either he will hate the one and love the other, or else he will be loyal to the one and despise the other.*
>
> — Matthew 6:24 (*The Bible – New King James Version*)

Inspiration is for Amateurs

Inspiration is for amateurs — the rest of us just show up and get to work.

— Chuck Close, painter

I write when I'm inspired, and I see to it that I'm inspired at nine o'clock every morning.

— Peter De Vries

You can't wait for inspiration. You have to go after it with a club.

— Jack London

If you want to write a book you must take your job seriously. You must show up and do the work, as the quotes above make clear.

I love Peter De Vries' comment best. He makes sure he is inspired at 9 a.m. every day. How awesome!

Inspiration does not magically bestow words to the writer. It's the other way around.

Inspiration rewards the consistent writer. Inspiration is the reward for your hard work. It does not flow down from Heaven as you sit there, waiting for angels to whisper in your ears.

Pablo Picasso nailed it when he said, "Inspiration exists, but it has to find you working."

Consistent writing allows your mind to connect the dots in your imagination. The more consistent, the more pathways to success your mind creates and the more prolific you become.

The inspiration myth is destructive and debilitating.

If you're a writer, the path forward is clear. Sit down at your desk, fire up your computer or grab your notepad and write.

Yes, it really is this simple.

With the destructive myth of inspiration out of the way, let's calculate how long it takes to write a book.

> *Whatever your hand finds to do, do it with your might.*
>
> — Ecclesiastes 9:10 (*The Bible – New King James Version*)

The Mathematics of Writing a Book

We've addressed the power of our mind, the power of focus, and we understand inspiration is the reward for hard work. Now let's examine what it takes to write a book, and discover why anyone can accomplish this quasi-Herculean task.

First, if your current daily word count is small, no problem. Do not allow your current word count to prevent you from finishing your book. No writer in history ever picked up a pen for the first time and wrote 2,000 words a day. We all start the same way - we write the words we can write every day - and improve our output over time.

> Do not despise these small beginnings, for the LORD rejoices to see the work begin…
>
> — Zechariah 4:10 (*The Bible, New Living Translation, 2nd Edition*)

Second, each genre has different recommended word counts and, even then, the correct length for your book still varies with every person you ask. Jacqui Murray, author and editor of over 100 books, lists a table of word counts for genres on her website.[3] While Murray's guide is excellent, for the purposes of this exercise I chose the count suggested by Chuck Sambuchino in his WritersDigest.com article *Word Count for Novels and Children's Books: The Definitive Post.*[4]

> *Between 80,000 and 89,999 words is a good range you should be aiming for. This is a 100% safe range for literary, mainstream, women's, romance, mystery, suspense, thriller and horror.*

The low end of Sambuchino's range says you must write 80,000 words to complete your book. How long it takes to write your book is up to you. You can write as fast or as slow as you choose, but you are not finished until you write 80,000 words. You control the deciding factor: how many words you write each day.

To determine how many days you require, use the formula:

TWR / WPD = N, where

TWR = Total Words Required to Complete your Novel.
WPD = How Many Words You Write Per Day.
N = Number of Days to Complete your Novel.

For example:

80,000 / 300 words per day = 267 days to complete your novel.

80,000 / 500 words per day = 160 days to complete your novel.

80,000 / 1,000 words per day = 80 days to complete your novel.

Double your daily word count and cut the time it takes to write your first draft in half.

80,000 / 2,000 words per day = 40 days to complete your novel.

Increase your output again by just 50% and you can write an entire first draft of a novel in a single month.

80,000 / 3,000 words per day = 27 days to complete your novel.

You can take as many years as you want to write your novel, but there is no unwritten rule saying you *must* take a long time.

The word counts and days to complete your book represent the days you actually write, not calendar days in a row, which brings me to my next point… counting the cost.

"For which of you, intending to build a tower, does not sit down first and count the cost, whether he has enough to finish it…"

— Luke 14:28 (*The Bible – New King James Version*)

Here is a small sampling of famous books and their word counts:[5]

1. The Color Purple by Alice Walker - 66,556
2. The Sun Also Rises by Ernest Hemingway - 67,707
3. Crime and Punishment by Fyodor Dostoyevsky - 211,591
4. Walden by Henry David Thoreau - 114,634
5. Slaughterhouse-Five by Kurt Vonnegut - 49,459
6. The Adventures of Huck Finn by Mark Twain - 109,571
7. The Picture of Dorian Gray by Oscar Wilde - 78,462
8. Fahrenheit 451 by Ray Bradbury - 46,118
9. The Martian Chronicles by Ray Bradbury - 64,768
10. War and Peace by Leo Tolstoy - 587,287

Practice Makes Perfect

The scariest moment is always just before you start.

— Stephen King

Fortune favors the bold, the old adage tells us, and this applies to writers. Only with bold and diligent effort can you achieve your goal. The best road to improvement is to write every day. Daily practice hones your skill and guarantees your success. The more you write, the more you learn.

One pervasive myth insists writing slow delivers good quality drafts and its inverse, writing fast results in poor quality drafts.

Complete hogwash. I argue the opposite. The faster you write, the more immersed you are in the creative process; the deeper your commitment to transfer the words from your mind onto the page. This prevents your Infernal Editor from overwhelming the process, a serious dilemma when you write slow.

There is one simple way to increase your writing speed and your daily word count.

Write every day. Write for longer every day.

Make the commitment, here and now, to write every single day. Set aside time to write every day and stick to it. The formation of every new habit feels difficult at first, but the more you do it, the easier it becomes.

The bonus, at least in my own experience, is the more I write, the more enjoyment I derive from writing. If you're like me, even in the slightest, you write because you can't NOT write. You are compelled to spew words onto the page by some unseen force within your mind.

My failure to write each day is painful, excruciating at times, yet the harsh truth is this - on those days when I do not dump the words out of my mind onto the page, the only person stopping me is me.

"The fault, dear Brutus, is not in our stars, but in ourselves..." [6]

Write every day. It's the best plan to finish your book. The more time you practice every day, the faster you become. In other words, you dump more words onto the page in less and less time.

"But what if I can only write on weekends?" you ask.

I would argue this: Then you don't value writing.

Harsh? Perhaps, but let me explain why I take this position. If writing your book is as important as you say it is, make the time to write. Of the 1,440 minutes you receive every day, I know you can squeeze out 15 minutes to write.

Make a solemn vow and keep your word. Carve out 15 minutes and write every day.

Commitment. There's your key. Now pick it up and unlock the door to your future.

Writing every day builds the habit of writing. Over time you write better, write more words per hour and write faster than you do today. Yes, even if you just write 15 minutes per day.

> *In all labor there is profit, but idle chatter leads only to poverty.*
>
> — Proverbs 14:23 (*The Bible – New King James Version*)

Personal Responsibility Will Change Your Life

The moment you take responsibility for everything in your life is the moment you can change *anything* in your life.

— Hal Elrod

Nobody wants to take responsibility for their actions or worse, their lack of action. The sad reality is your writing career changes when, and only when, you take responsibility for your decisions and your actions.

Make the commitment to write every single day for the next 30 days. Today is Day 1. Grab your calendar and a pen. Mark today's date Day 1 on your calendar. Count 30 days forward and mark it Day 30.

Make the commitment to write every single day, from Day 1 to Day 30, and build the bulletproof foundation for your writing life, even if its just 100 words per day.

Will it be easy?

Nope. I'd be lying to you if I said otherwise. What I can guarantee is the road ahead is simple.

That's the good news. It is simple.

The bad news is simple doesn't mean easy.

There is no magic to writing a book. None. You take action, every single day, until your book is finished. You plan, schedule and execute the plan. You write.

Focus, determination and self-discipline are your allies. Use them.

> *And whatever you do, do it heartily...*
>
> — Colossians 3:23 (*The Bible – New King James Version*)

Make a Decision... Follow it with Action

The most difficult thing is the decision to act, the rest is merely tenacity. Fears are paper tigers. You can do anything you decide to do.

— Amelia Earhart

I love Earhart's quote because tenacity is one of my strengths. Once I decide on a course of action, very little stops me from achieving my goal. My tenacity does not mean I'm unaffected by the demons plaguing you.

Fear, self-doubt, my Infernal Editor's insistence I'm still little more than a hack incapable of a coherent sentence, despite decades of practice. They all attack me daily, just as they attack you.

I just ignore my demons, every single one of them. They are the incoherent hacks, not me.

To ignore your demons and accomplish your goals, follow these five steps.

1. Decide what you want to accomplish.
2. Determine the most effective plan to achieve it.
3. Set a deadline to achieve this goal.
4. Parse your plan and set mini-deadlines for each step of the process.
5. Work your plan, one step at a time, until completed.

Any goal worth achieving follows the same path. Yes, that includes your finished book.

While you may break your goal into many smaller steps achieve it, your focus never changes. Invest your time and energy daily to your plan.

"It is in your moments of decision that your destiny is shaped."

Anthony Robbins is correct.

Make the decision to write every day. Follow your decision with action. Sit down and write every day, without exception.

> "Whatever you can do or dream you can, begin it. Boldness has genius, power and magic in it. Begin it now."

But you must make your decision…

Take Action, Part 1

Grab your notebook and pen and write down your answers to the following questions:

1. Define, in clear language, your writing goal. What do you want to accomplish? Write a daily blog post? Finish your non-fiction book, novel or screenplay?

2. Write down every step required to accomplish your goal. You can always add to this later, so don't beat yourself up with the idea your list must be perfect.

3. Choose a specific date to achieve your goal. Mark it on your calendar.

Take Action, Part 2

This is an eye-opening experience.

For the next seven days, document how much time you spend doing the things you do each day. At the end of the week, total up the number of minutes you spend on each item. Include work, sleep, commuting to and from work, watching television, social media. Your goal is to document your actions and how long they take for seven consecutive days.

The Awaken Your Author Mindset Workbook

If you prefer working from a physical workbook, here are two options:

1. Purchase the workbook from Amazon.com at:

https://ChristopherDiArmani.net/author-mindset-workbook

2. Download the workbook PDF from:

https://ChristopherDiArmani.net/author-foundations-workbook

Chapter 2

Define and Set Your Goals

What is a Goal?

To achieve your goal, you must first define it. Before you can define your goal, you must understand what the word means.

The dictionary defines goal as:

1. the object of a person's ambition or effort; an aim or desired result.
2. an aim or purpose
3. the end we direct our efforts toward
4. an observable and measurable end result achieved within a fixed time-frame.

Paraphrased for writers, a published book is our *chief aim or purpose*, and *we direct our ambition and effort to achieve it within a fixed time-frame.*

While the ultimate goal may seem overwhelming, especially in light of our deadline, when we define every action required to achieve it and attach a deadline to each step, we transform our sense of overwhelm and belief "*That's impossible*" into "*I can do this. I can make this happen.*"

When we create this new belief, we empower ourselves. When we define each task of the process and apply realistic deadlines to each one, we know with certainty what we must accomplish every day to achieve success..

For example, the goal of writing a book is intimidating when you write it as a single sentence, no matter how well-defined.

I write a complete novel by December 31.

When you break the goal into its smaller component goals, each with its own hard deadline, writing a book becomes manageable, believable and achievable.

I complete my book outline by January 31.

I complete my first draft by June 30 by writing 500 words per day.

I complete the second draft of my novel by September 30 by rewriting 900 words per day.

I design my book title and cover artwork by October 30.

I complete the final draft of my novel by December 31 by editing 1,400 words per day.

When we split our objective into its component parts, we transform the idea of writing a book from daunting and overwhelming into a series of easily-accomplished tasks.

Precision is Key

To be effective, your written goal must be:

1. Specific
2. Measurable
3. Achievable
4. Realistic
5. Time-Bound
6. Challenging

Example:

I write 500 words each day for 30 days.

The goal is defined with precision. The desired aim or purpose is to write 500 words each day.

It's measurable. Either you write 500 words each day or you do not. If you do, you achieve your goal. If not, you fail.

Achievable? Absolutely. Anyone can write 500 words per day, but you must commit to your decision and do the work. You must embrace this challenge daily and not shy away from it, ever.

Realistic? Yes, it is possible to write 500 words per day, even if you are not capable of it today.

Time-bound? Yes.

The writer accomplishes this feat every day for 30 consecutive days.

Challenging? That depends upon the writer, his or her daily habits, work, family and social commitments. If 500 words is too easy, raise the goal to 1,000. If it's too hard, cut it back to 300.

For best results, set a goal to push you slightly out of your comfort zone. Force yourself to stretch your writer's wings further each day.

If you easily write 500 words per day, pump up your daily word count to 750. If you struggle to achieve your new target, great. Strive to meet your ambitious goal and discover how easy it becomes within a short period of time.

The more you confront the limits of "possible" for yourself, the more you build your writing muscles and the stronger they become.

For example, when I could write 4,000 words per day six days in a row, I raised the bar. I challenged myself to write 5,000 words per day, a goal I achieved a short time later. My current goal is to write 8,000 words per day. I'm not there yet, but my goal is defined with precision, I designed a plan to achieve it, and I work every day to increase my daily word count.

Can I write 8,000 words per day consistently? Absolutely. There is no doubt in my mind. My belief 8,000 words per day is both possible and achievable creates my desire and, by extension, the self-discipline necessary to do the work every day.

Only when I push myself out of my comfort zone, beyond what is possible today, do I discover my genuine capabilities.

The same is true for you.

I do, however, offer two caveats.

Caveat #1: Every writer is different.

What is hard for me may be simple for you, or vice versa. Never judge your accomplishments by the bar set by another writer. Judge yourself against your accomplishments alone. Push yourself to stretch beyond your personal best every day.

CAVEAT #2: Every writing project is different.

I can write some projects only when the sun shines. Others I can write with ease, no matter the time of day (or night).

I could only write one project between the hours of 10pm and 4am.

If you find it difficult to write a specific project at a specific time, walk away from it for 6 hours, then start again. Search until you find the sweet spot, the time you write best for this project.

Don't be shocked if the answer you find is a little crazy, as I did, and you're a possessed demon writing from 10 p.m. until 4 a.m. every night. If it can happen to me, it just might happen to you too! The important takeaway is this - be open to all possibilities to put your words on the page.

Action Step

Define your writing goal using the six traits listed above. Your goal may be to write a specific number of words per day or to complete your first draft by a specific date. Whatever your goal, write it down in present tense, using clear and concise language.

Failure Is Not An Option

Incorporate the belief *failure is not an option* into your life. Take a page from No Limit Holdem and *go all in*. Hold nothing back. Unless you go all in, until you make success your only option, you always find a way to wiggle out of your commitment. Human nature defaults to the easy road, the path of least resistance. It's a universal human failing. It guarantees mediocrity and failure, never success.

When you wiggle out of your commitments, especially those made to yourself, the only person who loses is you. Why? Because nobody else on Earth cares if you complete your book - not your mother, your father, your husband or your wife. Nobody.

Go all in. Burn the bridge behind you. Ensure a retreat to your former safe and comfortable existence is no longer possible.

According to legend, when a high-level Soviet spy wanted to defect to America, he gave a letter to a trusted friend, along with instructions to deliver his letter to the authorities at 5pm. The letter confessed he was a traitor, an American spy.

He burned the bridge of retreat. He could not return to his old life, even if his nerve failed. The fact the letter would be delivered, no matter what, gave him the courage and strength of will necessary to follow through with the plan. Whether he stayed or the authorities captured him as he attempted to defect, the result was the same - he would be killed.

Failure was no longer an option.

Whether the story is true or not is irrelevant. It makes a valid point. We must commit to our path without reservation.

The day I quit my six-figure job to write full time my emotions bounced between elation, despair, terror and all points in between. First, elation because I was now free to follow my passion, not fulfill someone else's dreams; despair and terror because I just tossed away a six-figure income to write.

It was the correct decision, despite my conflicting emotions. By quitting the job, I forced myself into a corner. Success as a writer was no longer just a nice idea - it was my only option.

No, I'm not saying you must quit your day job and write full time, just because I did. That is absurd. The decision to quit my job when I did was the correct one for me, at the time. Two years earlier it was not.

Find out what makes your life content and comfortable, but unfulfilling, then shred it into tiny little pieces.

Force your hand.

You want to write a book? Great. Drive yourself to take every action required, no matter how difficult, to achieve your goal.

If it means you must cut the cable and sell your television, do it. The more drastic the measure, the better. Action proves commitment, so take action. Yes, right now.

Make the decision failure, as a writer, is no longer an option. Burn every bridge of retreat. Sever the road to your cozy and familiar sanctuary because one day, when your nerve fails you, when your determination and self-discipline abandons you, there must be no other option.

On this day you must know, deep in your heart, you must write.

On this day you must place one foot in front of the other.

It's a bold step. It's a brave and terrifying step, but when you know in your heart you are 100% committed, life gets incredibly simple.

All your worry and fear drops away.

Why?

There's nothing left to worry about, nothing left to fear.

You know the path forward. You know every single step you must take. You know when you must finish.

All that remains is for you to do the work.

Simple.

Chapter 3

Self-Honesty: Your Starting Point

Honesty is the Best Medicine

Facing reality is hard, never more so than when we examine our own motivations, or worse, the lack thereof.

Without knowledge of where we are today, it is impossible to map our way to success. Before we can change our creative life for the better, we must evaluate our current state.

Self-honesty is key.

The only yardstick is you.

Don't compare yourself to anyone else or their accomplishments. They don't matter, nor do their achievements.

When you honestly examine your life you must admit one unassailable fact - if you do not schedule time to write, you do not write. It simply doesn't get done.

That's one crappy thought. Once you face it head-on and accept it, the solution is as simple as it is profound.

Schedule time to write every day and keep your appointment.

"But," you cry, "I don't have time!"

Sure you do.

You begin each day with the same 1,440 minutes I do.

You have time.

Your sole decision is this:

What activity or activities will you give up to make more time for writing?

Determine Your Current Writing Speed

You cannot learn to write faster when you do not know how many words you write per hour today. If you want to write more words per hour, complete the exercise below and determine your baseline.

This is way more fun than it sounds, I promise.

Action Step

Set a 15-minute countdown timer on your smartphone. Why 15 minutes? Five minutes is far too short for an accurate assessment. Ten minutes is good, but ultimately misleading, based on my experience.

I cannot explain how or why, but I write twice as many words in 15 minutes as I write in 10.

I agree… It makes no sense. None whatsoever, yet my results remained constant no matter how many times I ran this test, hence my recommendation to set your timer for 15 minutes.

If you don't have a smart phone app, try these alternatives:

https://tomato-timer.com/

https://ChristopherDiArmani.net/free-pomodoro-writing-timer

(*My free Pomodoro Timer for Windows*)

Start the timer.

Write for 15 minutes, uninterrupted. It doesn't matter what you write, so long as you write until the timer expires.

No, you cannot skip this step. It's the very bedrock upon which you will build your foundation.

At the end of the 15 minutes, write down your word count. This is your baseline.

Run this test again. Record your results.

In fact, I recommend you complete this exercise three times, using three different prompts, to see if your results vary based on what you write. You probably won't see any change but, if there is a disparity, see if you can pin down what causes you to write more or write less in your tests. I'd love to hear your results.

Writing Prompts

If you need a writing prompt for this exercise, choose one from the list below. Alternately, use one of the online writing prompt generators listed in the Resources chapter at the end of the book.

1. You discover your friend harbors a secret.
2. Someone stabs you in your dreams. You wake up to discover it wasn't a dream.
3. You overheard a conversation and can't get it out of your mind.
4. Describe meeting your greatest love.
5. What is the one thing you cannot live without?
6. The garden was overgrown now.
7. What did the last person to praise you say?
8. Describe the most fragile object you held in your hands.
9. Describe your worst sports nightmare.
10. You wake up to the sound of a dog barking.

Chapter 4

Resistance to Change in Yourself and Others

Change is Required

The secret of change is to focus all of your energy, not on fighting the old, but on building the new.

— Socrates

To complete your novel this year, you must change. This is not news. You already know it in your heart, if not your head. I say this because:

1. You bought this book. If the idea of finishing your book didn't overwhelm you, you'd be writing it instead of reading this sentence.
2. You struggle to make writing a priority in your life.
3. You struggle to find the time, energy and focus necessary to write.
4. Your current plan of action failed. It does not work. Your book isn't finished (or worse, you haven't started). You can't even see an obvious path to get there.

You want to complete your manuscript and publish your book. To achieve this result, you must change your approach. Obvious, right?

But changing your approach brings up two more issues.

1. Your own internal resistance to change, and
2. The resistance of others to the change you want to make.

The first issue, your own internal resistance to change, is relatively easy to deal with. You control the decision. Once you accept where you are right now and understand, deep in your soul, it is not where you want to be, your internal resistance drops away like a Persian cat shedding its fur.

The second issue is more difficult, but only a little. It appears harder to cope with, but the resistance you encounter in others is just a reflection of your own. Their resistance challenges your resolve, determination and desire to achieve your goal. You are more powerful than these external forces, I assure you, as the story below proves.

When I quit my full-time job to devote myself to writing, I'd be lying if I said it was easy. I needed to overcome my own desire to procrastinate. Once I beat my own demon into submission I still needed to deal with my wife's desire to spend all day with me, since I was at home.

We needed to balance both needs - her need to spend quality time with her husband and my need to write every day - by setting boundaries. At heart, human beings are little kids who hate being told "No." Nobody appreciates boundaries.

If I wanted to write effectively and productively each day (I did) my wife and I needed to establish clear boundaries.

On my side, the boundary became "If my office door is closed, I am not to be disturbed."

On her side, it was "Your door can't stay closed all day."

My wife's interruptions challenged me to become focused and committed to writing. The instant I accepted her unspoken challenge and took my commitment to write seriously, her resistance melted away.

Setting boundaries produced an interesting side effect in my life and in our marriage. When my office door is closed, I am compelled to write. I feel an urgency to get the job done. Otherwise, my closed door disrespects both my wife and my commitment to her. She respects my door is only closed when necessary and she honors my need for uninterrupted writing time.

Both our needs are met.

I close the door when I need uninterrupted creative time, but leave it open otherwise. I take breaks to visit with her, to take a walk and share our day.

Challenging, at first, but ultimately far more rewarding for each of us individually and for our marriage.

The Seven Commandments of the Writing Life

There are seven duties a writer must accomplish every single day. These are not polite suggestions. Consider them Commandments issued from God Himself, if that makes them easier to swallow.

They apply to all professional writers. If you want to write a book, they apply to you too.

1. Write every day

You must stay drunk on writing so reality cannot destroy you.

— Ray Bradbury, Zen in the Art of Writing

2. Read from a book in your chosen genre every day

I kept always two books in my pocket, one to read, one to write in.

— Robert Louis Stevenson

3. Read from a writing craft book every day

If you don't have time to read, you don't have the time (or the tools) to write. Simple as that.

— Stephen King

4. Set a goal with a hard deadline

Find out the reason that commands you to write; see whether it has spread its roots into the very depth of your heart; confess to yourself you would have to die if you were forbidden to write.

— Rainer Maria Rilke

5. Push the personal boundaries of what you believe is possible

If my doctor told me I had only six minutes to live, I wouldn't brood. I'd type a little faster.

— Isaac Asimov

6. Commit to your path.

Desire is the key to motivation, but it's determination and commitment to an unrelenting pursuit of your goal – a commitment to excellence – that will enable you to attain the success you seek.

— Mario Andretti

7. Develop courage

Courage is the commitment to begin without any guarantee of success.
— Johan Wolfgang von Goethe

You know what you must do. You know the action you must take, but the *doing*, isn't that always the problem?

The Distance Between Should and Do

Don't be a writer; be writing.

— William Faulkner

There is no distance greater than the one between should and do. Writers know what we *should* do to write our book, yet we don't do it. We say we will try. We lie to ourselves.

To quote Yoda, "Try not. Do… or do not. There is no try."

You cannot try to write every day. You either write or you do not. All the excuses in the universe cannot transform our desire to write into words on the page.

Action is the way forward.

Everything else is meaningless.

Success is Terrifying

I went for years not finishing anything. Because, of course, when you finish something you can be judged.

— Erica Jong

Fear of success stops most writers in their tracks, me included. On the bright side, after I achieved some small measure of success, this fear isn't my most pressing one. On the downside, others moved in to take its place.

I'm a member of a couple writing communities on Facebook and, in one of those groups, a young woman shared her apprehension about publishing her first book. Her primary fear was of failure - she was afraid nobody would read her book.

I asked her, "Who is reading your book now?"

"Nobody," came her timid reply.

"What is there to be afraid of?" I asked. "Nobody's reading your book right now. You're already living your worst-case scenario, so if just one person buys your book, that's an improvement, right?"

She published her book the next day.

Only by facing our fears do we learn if they are valid.

They seldom are...

Change is Scary

Often, the greater our ignorance about something, the greater our resistance to change.

— Marc Bekoff

Change is scary.

In my own life, nothing good ever lands in my lap by accident. I must change something first. Or, expressed with brutal honesty, the discomfort of my refusal to change forces me to do what I resist. This change, in turn, delivers the positive benefits I desire. One might expect I'd get the memo by now. Nope, I'm a slow learner.

Nobody likes change. It forces us out of our comfort zone, and we LOVE our comfort zone. It's cozy. The pillows are big and soft. We know the people and how they respond to any given situation.

It's *familiar*.

If that's not a pox on the creative mind, I don't know what is.

Only when I forced myself out of my comfort zone did I publish my book. It reached #1 in its category on Amazon.

Only when I forced myself out of my comfort zone did I write an entire non-fiction book of 55,000 words in 15 days.

Only when I forced myself out of my comfort zone did I write a 106,600 word first draft of a fiction novel in 29 days.

The benefits, the rewards I receive when I force myself out of my comfort zone are documented above. Those are just three in a long list of pretty awesome accomplishments. None of them could happen until I changed my ways.

I needed to face my fears and, I assure you, your fears are mine and mine are yours. So, let's deal with them right here, right now.

Fears to Overcome

Life isn't about waiting for the storm to pass; it's about learning to dance in the rain. It's about removing the fear in this area of your life so you can focus on what matters most.

— Anthony Robbins, Money: Master the Game

A writer's life is nothing, if not riddled with fears. So many of those fears are self-induced and self-perpetuating. Nevertheless, they must be overcome on our road to success. Fear is a roadblock. Nothing more, nothing less.

The real trouble is we create those roadblocks ourselves.

We pull over to the side of the road, stop the car, turn off the engine and wait for someone to come along and save us.

Here's the thing. The entire premise is false. Help is not just around the corner. No hero is waiting around the corner to save us from our fears. Nobody else even knows we suffer, let alone care about our pain.

William Kenower may have a valid point with what he calls "*The Mother of All Fears.*"[7]

> What other people think of what I write is more important than what I think of what I write.
>
> What makes this particular fear so seductive is its apparent practicality. It seems practical because we are not just writers; we are authors. It doesn't matter whether you have published thirty New York Times best-selling novels or have just sat down to begin your memoir. If you have ever shared even one thing you have written with another person, you are an author. The moment you surrender this thing you wrote in the supreme privacy of your imagination to the unknown of another person's mind, your relationship to your writing changes. You are no longer writing in your journal or diary.

Now this poem or story or essay is destined for another human heart, and every author quickly understands that he has no control whatsoever over what occurs when that other human heart receives it.

Here are just some of the many fears writers face:

Fear of success

- Fear of failure
- Fear of shame
- Fear of self-delusion
- Fear we lack talent
- Fear we will look foolish
- Fear we have nothing to say
- Fear nobody cares about what we have to say
- Fear we lack life experience
- Fear we lack writing experience
- Fear we lack education
- Fear of rejection
- Fear of starting
- Fear of finishing
- Lack of time
- Lack of money
- Fear of being alone

The list, as I said, is far from complete, but truth slays fear, so let's apply a little truth to the matter, shall we?

> *For God has not given us a spirit of fear, but of power and of love and of a sound mind.*
>
> — 2 Timothy 1:7 (The Bible – New King James Version)

The Nike Challenge

We are all faced with a series of great opportunities brilliantly disguised as impossible situations.

— Charles R. Swindoll

Just Do It.

Nike's marketing slogan epitomizes the foundation principle of success.

You must do something.

Let these three words become our mantra, our truth.

Become unstoppable.

Just do it.

Action Step

Write out your answers to these questions:

1. How many of the Seven Commandments of the Writing Life do you perform each day?

2. How many of these fears apply to you?

3. Are there other fears you experience not on this list? If so, write them down, too.

4. Do you want to become unstoppable?

5. List all your excuses for why you can't write today. List every thought, excuse, reason and rationalization for not writing, no matter how silly it appears to you.

6. List all the outside forces that hold you back from writing. Include everything - your job, your family, any commitments you have to volunteer organizations, everything. If it sucks up time you'd rather be writing, it must be on this list.

Chapter 5

Three Steps to Prolific Writing

Make a Decision

When you consistently make better choices you create better habits. These better habits produce better character. When you have better character, you add more value to the world. When you become more valuable, you attract bigger and better opportunities. This allows you to make more of a contribution in your life. This in turn leads to bigger and better results.

— Jack Canfield, The Power Of Focus

Nothing changes in your life until you make the decision to change it.

Nothing.

What is a decision?

1. The act of or need for making up one's mind.

2. A choice of what should be done after considering all available possibilities.

3. A conclusion or resolution reached after consideration.

4. A determination arrived at after consideration.

Make the decision to write every single day.

Then do it.

Make a Commitment

Commitment allows you to focus intently on a few highly important goals and achieve a greater degree of success than you otherwise would.
— Mark Mason, The Subtle Art of Not Giving a F*ck

Commitment means:

1. the state of being dedicated to an activity.
2. an engagement or obligation that restricts freedom of action.
3. a willingness to give your time and energy to something you believe in, or a promise or firm decision to do something.
4. the act of binding yourself (intellectually or emotionally) to a course of action.
5. A pledge or undertaking.

Commit yourself to the decision you made. Write every single day.

Take Action

Small deeds done are better than great deeds planned.
— Peter Marshall

When I say, "Take action," what do I mean? Action is defined as the process of doing something, typically to achieve an aim.

How many words must you write every day to achieve your goal by your deadline?

What must you write first, second and third?

Why are you still reading this? Why aren't you at your desk, writing?

It is better to write 100 words today, than promise to write 500 words tomorrow.

Deadlines are for Professionals

Efficient writers set deadlines. It's a professional necessity.

Always set a deadline, no matter what you are writing - blog post, email sequence, or book. In fact, the shorter and more urgent your deadline, the more powerful its effect upon you.

A deadline too far in the future holds no authority and a deadline one hour from now forces you into frenzied action. Neither are productive.

Always set realistic deadlines for yourself, but make them sooner than you are comfortable with. Always challenge yourself to achieve more in less time.

Be Dedicated

Your life does not get better by chance, it gets better by change.

— Jim Rohn

Dedicated is defined as:

1. self-sacrificing devotion and loyalty
2. the willingness to give a lot of time and energy to something because it is important

When we commit to our finished book by a specific deadline, we:

1. Make an obligation to ourselves and/or others to achieve this task on time.
2. Devote our time and energy to uphold our obligation to complete our book by our deadline.
3. Bind ourselves, both emotionally and intellectually, to this single course of action.
4. Restrict ourselves from doing those things, if done, interfere with our ability to complete our manuscript on time.
5. Allow nothing to stand between us and our daily writing sessions. We prove our dedication when we sacrifice time spent on less valuable activities (television, Youtube, video games, etc.) and devote it to writing, instead.

Commitment obligates us to do what we say we will do, when we must do it, to we reap the rewards we desire. It works best when we commit to others. We are far less willing to disappoint others than ourselves.

Yes, it's this simple and this hard.

If there was an easier way, I'd tell you.

Are you up for the challenge?

Excellent. Now let's schedule time to write.

Chapter 6

You Do Not Accomplish What You Do Not Schedule

Scheduling 101

Scheduling in three simple steps.

1. Make a list of all tasks you must complete.
2. Assign a time to begin each task.
3. Assign a deadline for each task.

Simple, right?

In the quest for higher word counts each day, information is your friend.

When you schedule time to write and track your word count for each session, you introduce accountability to your writing. This single change will probably double your writing output per month.

Louise, founder of SmallStepsGuide.co.uk[8], offers a free Excel spreadsheet designed to help you determine your most productive writing time of day. Note your start time, end time, and your word count for the session. After two weeks you'll learn a lot about your current writing habits and your most productive time of day to write.

Once you determine your most productive writing time with Louise's spreadsheet, go to your local Dollar Store and purchase a wall calendar. While you're there, grab a package of stickers: gold stars, thumbs up, smiley faces - whatever strikes your fancy. Hang your new calendar on the wall in front of your desk - after you schedule your writing sessions on it.

When you meet your word count goal each day, paste a sticker to the corresponding square on the calendar. This is a visual reflection of your commitment to write every day. Lots of stars in a row equals commitment. Blocks of empty space between the stars… not so much.

This also doubles as a reward system. We all love rewards, even those we give to ourselves. I award one gold star for each 1,000 words I write per day. It's a powerful visual indicator of my productivity.

Try it.

I can't speak for you, but I find an unbroken string of gold stars on my calendar is powerful and motivating. You may be pleasantly surprised how useful this silly reward is, and how important it becomes to see gold stars on every square of your calendar.

Action Step

Go to your local dollar store and purchase the following:

1. A hanging wall calendar.
2. An assortment of stickers.

Use the stickers to reward yourself every day you meet a specific writing goal, such as a daily minimum word count.

Chapter 7

The 7 Steps to Building a Fruitful Writing Life

Where are you now?

Before you can map the journey to your destination, you must know where you are.

Determine your daily word count.

Work to increase it, if only by 15 words per day. Baby steps still move you forward. In one week, this adds up to an extra 105 words. In a month, an additional 400 words.

Determine your goal and set a deadline.

Believe in Yourself

What we believe we achieve.

It's a cliché because it is true.

Your brain is the most powerful machine on the planet. Believe in your desire and ability to write. Nothing can stop you then. Write a positive affirmation to reinforce this new belief in yourself and your talent.

Be Honest With Yourself

Be honest about your abilities. Then set realistic goals for improvement.

The action steps throughout this book is your path to self-honesty.

If a physical workbook makes it easier for you, purchase one from your favorite book retailer.

If you prefer the free option (who doesn't?) download the workbook PDF from:

https://ChristopherDiArmani.net/author-foundations-workbook

Define and Set Your Goals

Define your goal with clarity and precision.

To be effective, a goal must be:

1. Specific.
2. Measurable.
3. Achievable.
4. Realistic.
5. Time-Bound.
6. Challenging.

Always challenge yourself to accomplish more than you feel comfortable with each day. It's the only way to discover your true capabilities and their limits. My bet is you never find the boundary of what's possible.

Make a Decision

Make the decision to write every day.

This is the most important resolution you can make to advance your writing career.

Combine your decision to write daily with a word count goal just beyond your current capability. When you achieve this word count consistently, increase it by 25% and keep going. In no time, your word count doubles or even triples.

Does this thought excite you? It should.

Commit Yourself To Your Decision

Action is proof of commitment. Decision without action is meaningless.

Commit to the action required to implement your decision every single day, without exception.

You and you alone are responsible for your daily word count. Nobody else can write your book. Nobody else wants to, nor do they care.

God hates a coward and rewards the brave, so be bold. Commit to your decision. Hold nothing back. Remember, failure is not an option.

Take the Actions Required

Take the action required to implement your decision. This is the proof stage of commitment.

If your decision is to write every day, then sit down at your computer and do it. Action breeds success. Discipline breeds habit. Your daily writing habit transforms you from an average writer into an unstoppable author.

It's all so simple, isn't it?

Dedicate Yourself to Completing Those Tasks Daily

Dedication and commitment come at a cost: you must sacrifice something else. Root out the things you value least in life and replace them with those you value most.

When you rid your life of the meaningless, your life explodes with happiness, success and achievement. For writers, this is powerful mojo indeed.

Schedule Each Task With a Deadline

A deadline is optimism on steroids.

No matter how big or how small, give every task on your to do list a deadline. Make the deadline uncomfortably short.

Mark every deadline on your calendar. Break it down into its smallest component parts, and set a deadline for each one of those as well.

Then beat your deadlines.

> The biggest thing separating people from their artistic ambitions is not a lack of talent. It's a lack of a deadline. Give someone an enormous task, a supportive community, and a friendly-yet-firm due date, and miracles will happen every time.
>
> — Chris Baty, NaNoWriMo founder[9]

The road ahead is defined. You built your roadmap to success.

Now, implement your plan of action.

Just do it.

I can't wait to read *everything* you write.

Christopher di Armani

Author Extraordinaire

Download the Free Workbook

The Plan for Success is Written on Paper

Research conducted by Dr. Gail Matthews[10] at the Dominican University of California confirmed the results of a never-performed, but oft-cited Harvard or Yale study on the power of written goals. The mythical study claimed only 3% of the graduating class wrote down their goals and 20 years later out-earned their classmates by over ten times.

While not quite so earth-shattering as multiplied earning power, Dr. Matthews' study confirms when you write down your goals you are more liable to follow through and achieve them.

When you take one simple action and write down your goals, you increase your likelihood to follow through on your commitment and take the actions necessary to achieve your goals.

Pretty simple, right? Obvious, even, yet so many people do not write down their goals. They *decrease* their chances for success out of sheer laziness.

That's crazy.

Download your free PDF copy of the Author Foundations Workbook. Complete every exercise to achieve greater clarity in your life and in every word you write.

https://ChristopherDiArmani.net/free-author-foundations-workbook

The Road to Success Begins With Your Morning Routine

There is no magic to productivity, just planning, scheduling and execution.

Everyone has a morning routine. Your alarm goes off. You wake up. You hop in the shower and get dressed. You eat breakfast and brush your teeth, then run out the door to work.

Not very uplifting.

What if you could start your day focused and productive, instead of waking up, coming to, and finally dragging your butt out the door to get to work on time? What if you could laser-focus your mind on your most important goal - a finished novel?

You can.

Read the second book in the Author Success Foundations series, *Design Your Morning Routine To Jump-Start Your Daily Writing Success* and learn how a few simple changes to how you start your day can reap massive benefits for the rest of it.

Available from your favorite online book retailers today.

For more information, visit:

https://ChristopherDiArmani.net/design-your-morning-routine

One Last Thing!

First, thank you for reading this book!

If you enjoyed this book and found it informative (and even if you did not) I would be grateful if you would post an honest review on Amazon and/or Goodreads. Every review helps this book find more readers, the lifeblood of any author.

http://ChristopherDiArmani.net/review-author-foundation-amazon

http://ChristopherDiArmani.net/review-author-foundations-goodreads

Your support in the form of an honest review really does make a difference. Reviews help authors sell more books and I read every one as part of my efforts to make my books even better.

I would also be grateful if you shared a link to this book on your social media accounts.

http://christopherdiarmani.net/book1-gplus

http://christopherdiarmani.net/book1-facebook

http://christopherdiarmani.net/book1-twitter

http://christopherdiarmani.net/book1-pinterest

http://christopherdiarmani.net/book1-goodreads

If, for some reason, you did not like this book or didn't get what you expected out of it please tell me directly. I will use your constructive criticism to fix any flaws in my book so it better meets your expectations. Please contact me here:

https://ChristopherDiArmani.net/Contact

Thank you so much for your support, feedback and your honest reviews.

Sincerely,

Christopher di Armani

Author Extraordinare

http://ChristopherDiArmani.net

About Christopher di Armani

"Author Extraordinaire"

Christopher di Armani is an Amazon bestselling author and the creator of Author Success Foundations.

This 7-book series teaches authors at any level how to develop the mindset, daily routines and work habits necessary to unleash their creativity and get their books published.

Christopher has published 16 books and produced 4 documentary films on topics ranging from the craft of writing to civil liberties and politics.

Download your free introduction to the Author Success Foundations series at:

https://ChristopherDiArmani.net/AuthorSuccessFoundations

Books by Christopher

Awaken Your Author Mindset: Finish Writing Your Book Fast (Author Success Foundations 1)

https://ChristopherDiArmani.net/author-mindset

https://ChristopherDiArmani.net/author-mindset-workbook

Learn how to develop your bullet-proof Author Mindset and create a system guaranteed to deliver success and to build the habits required to work this system every single day.

The choice is yours. If you continue to do what you've always done you'll just get what you already have, an unfinished manuscript and all the disappointment, discarded dreams and self-loathing you can handle.

You will never finish your book.

Now, imagine the possible…

Allow me to be your guide to help you construct a mindset, a solid foundation to complete your manuscript so published becomes, not just possible, but inevitable. This is the power of the Author Mindset.

Design Your Morning Routine: Jump-Start Your Writing Success (Author Success Foundations Book 2)

https://ChristopherDiArmani.net/morning-routine

https://ChristopherDiArmani.net/morning-routine-workbook

There is no magic to writing a book. None. You take action, every single day, until your book is finished. You plan, schedule and execute the plan. You write.

If you are serious about finishing your manuscript, grab your notebook, a pen, and a cup of your favorite beverage, and join me at the kitchen table. We'll chat about habits, willpower and self-discipline. We'll discuss how the mind functions, what makes a habit stick, and how our willpower fades throughout the day. We'll talk about concrete steps to improve your self-discipline.

Then I'll ask you to complete a series of exercises. These exercises reveal, at a deep level, what's important to you - what you value most in life. This clarity of purpose allows you to create a morning routine designed to jump-start your daily writing output.

Author Focus: Develop Your Author Vision Statement and Laser-Focus Your Writing Career (Author Success Foundations Book 3)

https://ChristopherDiArmani.net/author-focus

https://ChristopherDiArmani.net/author-focus-workbook

Writing is easy. Finishing your book is easy, too.

Focus. Be diligent. Apply self-discipline and determination.

You already possess these qualities. This book would not appeal to you if you didn't.

Your author vision statement is an extraordinary targeting mechanism to guide you to your ultimate destination - the end of Publication Highway.

The exercises ahead serve one purpose - to focus your mind on what you value most - your published book.

Join me and map your personal journey down Publication Highway. Discover what you value most, not just in writing, but in your entire life.

Isn't your ideal future worth the time?

Prolific Author: The Step-by-Step Guide to Write More Words in Less Time and Finish Your Book Fast (Author Success Foundations 4)

https://ChristopherDiArmani.net/prolific-author

https://ChristopherDiArmani.net/prolific-author-workbook

The key to unlock your drive to succeed is knowing why you write. When you understand how your desire to write fulfills your core needs, you transform writing from a chore to be dreaded into the vision you were born to fulfill. Time set aside to write becomes as critical to your life as the food you eat and the water you drink.

If we believe success does not matter, neither does the road we travel to get there.

Success matters. The road you travel to achieve success matters more.

Your daily writing routine is the last piece of the puzzle to build a life focused on accomplishing your goal - a finished and published book.

Done is Better than Perfect: 7 Keys to Finish Writing Your Book Fast (Author Success Foundations 5)

https://ChristopherDiArmani.net/done-better-perfect

Give Up Your Perfectionism and Publish Your Book

The three fundamental truths of writing are:

1. Your book will never be perfect.
2. You cannot publish what you do not complete.
3. Done is better than perfect.

Learn how to finish your book easier, faster and better than you ever thought possible when you apply the Seven Keys of Writing Success.

Become Unstoppable: 7 Habits of Highly Successful Authors (Author Success Foundations Book 6)

https://ChristopherDiArmani.net/become-unstoppable

Success leaves clues.

Figure out what successful authors did to advance their careers, then do what they did. It's the most effective course of action. Simple concept, but we must do the work. You know, the hard part.

In the pages ahead I discuss how each habit works, as well as the lies we tell ourselves to rationalize our lack of forward progress. Finally, I shine the light of truth on the lies we tell ourselves and watch as they scurry away like little cockroaches.

Apply these principles to your life and you'll achieve their success. It's inevitable. All it takes is a pinch of perseverance, a dash of focus, and two cups of hard work.

I Don't Have Time To Write And Other Lies Writers Tell Themselves (Author Success Foundations Book 7)

https://ChristopherDiArmani.net/no-time-to-write

Stop Lying To Yourself.

In this installment of the Author Success Foundations series, I dissect seven lies writers tell ourselves and shine the light of truth upon each one.

Every falsehood obscures a truth we refuse to confront. The job of a writer, any writer, is to face our fears head on, protected by the body armor of honesty and integrity. Only then does the brilliance we etch on the page shine bright for the world to see.

Each delusion corrodes holes in our armor, holes the insidious demons of worry, self-doubt, procrastination and perfectionism slip through to poison us.

The Author Success Foundations series provides the tools and materials to patch those holes, to reinforce and strengthen our armor. The day of battle is here, and we must march ever forward. If we stop, even for a moment, our words shrink under the oppressive heat of our fears and we fail.

Step inside. Face your fears. Show these pathetic demons you cannot be cowed. Own your internal dialog and reshape it into a powerful engine, then use that power to drive down Publication Highway.

The Simple 3-Step Secret to Slaughter Writer's Block And Vanquish it Forever

https://ChristopherDiArmani.net/Writers-Block-Book

There is no more perfect Hell than one where I cannot write. You know that terror, too, don't you? That sense your last remaining creative spark abandoned you some time back. It's sickening.

Let me show you how to extricate yourself from that "perfect Hell" permanently.

TOP SECRET - Inspiration, Motivation and Encouragement - 701 Essential Quotes for Writers

https://ChristopherDiArmani.net/Top-Secret-Quotes

This compilation of 701 quotes delivers inspiration, motivation and encouragement on 39 aspects of writing and the writing life.

You will discover quotes to make you laugh and quotes to make you cry. Some are familiar, like old friends. Others you will meet for the first time. All have a common theme: The Writing Life.

When you need it most, you will find words of encouragement here.

Filming Police is Legal - How to Hold Police Accountable While Staying Out of Jail

I write about police issues regularly. I highlight good cops when I can, but I focus on the problems in our police forces with honesty, integrity and abuse. Every time news breaks about police seizing another citizen's camera or cell phone I receive the same question.

Christopher, is it legal to film police?

The unequivocal answer is a court-affirmed YES. It is legal to film police in every state in the United States of America and in every single province and territory of Canada. That YES comes with specific caveats for the audio portion of a recording depending upon your jurisdiction, and it is critical you know those caveats.

The purpose of this book is to educate mere citizens and police forces alike about the legality of the right of citizens to film police, along with an examination of the legal history supporting our legal right to do so.

https://ChristopherDiArmani.net/Filming-Police

Justin Trudeau - 47 Character-Revealing Quotes from Canada's 23rd Prime Minister and What They Mean for You

On October 19, 2015 Canadians elected their 23rd Prime Minister based on good looks, nice hair and a famous name.

They voted for style over substance.

Our 23rd Prime Minister's entire leadership experience consisted of teaching snowboarding lessons and high school drama. His management experience consisted of administering his trust fund and his ego.

Not a single thought was given to what he stood for, what his party stood for, or what he would actually do once elected to the highest office in the land. That bothered me. That bothered me so much I began to research his much-publicized missteps and that in turn revealed a disturbing pattern within Trudeau's numerous faux pas. That pattern is the focus of this book.

https://ChristopherDiArmani.net/Justin-Trudeau-Book-1

From Refugee to Cabinet Minister: Maryam Monsef's Meteoric Rise to Power and her Spectacular Fall From Grace

Maryam Monsef is the ultimate immigrant success story. She could not speak English when she arrived in Canada at age eleven. Two decades later she became Canada's first Muslim Cabinet Minister.

Maryam Monsef's story begins with her mother, a young Afghan widow who fled Afghanistan for Canada with her three young daughters in 1995. That widow spoke English but her three daughters did not. They brought something far more valuable to Canada: the unshakeable belief they could accomplish anything they wanted, so long as they worked hard.

It's no accident her belief in herself led Maryam Monsef to a Cabinet post. She worked hard to learn English and graduated from Trent University, an impossible accomplishment in her native Afghanistan.

Maryam Monsef became the unwitting scapegoat for Trudeau's broken promise on electoral reform, a promise he knew he would break by May 2016. Her birthplace controversy, her attempts to discredit and insult her electoral reform committee, combined with the Prime Minister's betrayal of her trust, sounded the death knell of her political career.

This, then, is the story of one young woman's meteoric rise to political power. It is also the story of that young woman's undoing at the hands of a narcissistic and self-serving celebrity feminist, Justin Trudeau.

https://ChristopherDiArmani.net/Maryam-Monsef-Book

Appendix - Free Resources

Writing Timers
- https://tomato-timer.com/
- https://ChristopherDiArmani.net/free-pomodoro-writing-timer

Reference
- https://www.powerthesaurus.org/
- http://www.merriam-webster.com/
- The Elements of Style Free Kindle Edition
  https://www.amazon.com/dp/B005IT0V8O/

Scheduling
- https://www.vertex42.com/calendars/quarterly-calendar.html
- http://www.smallstepsguide.co.uk/track-your-time/

Writing Tools
- http://www.hemingwayapp.com/
- https://www.grammarly.com/
- https://www.libreoffice.org/
- http://www.spacejock.com/yWriter6.html
- http://stevenluzern.org/product/hypnosis-creative-writing/

Writing Prompt Generators
- http://writingexercises.co.uk/quick-plot-generator.php
- http://writingexercises.co.uk/plotgenerator.php
- http://writingexercises.co.uk/take-three-nouns.php
- http://writingexercises.co.uk/dialogue-generator.php
- http://writingexercises.co.uk/subjectgenerator.php

⇨ https://thestoryshack.com/tools/writing-prompt-generator/

⇨ http://www.seventhsanctum.com/generate.php?Genname=writeprompt

⇨ https://www.buzzfeed.com/danieldalton/go-go-nanowrimo?utm_term=.dgWv1vBkW#.lakKvK7aj

⇨ http://www.springhole.net/writing_roleplaying_randomators/fairytaleplot.htm

⇨ http://www.springhole.net/writing_roleplaying_randomators/character-obstacles.htm

⇨ http://www.springhole.net/writing_roleplaying_randomators/character-bonding-moment.htm

⇨ http://www.springhole.net/writing_roleplaying_randomators/creepypastaplot.htm

⇨ http://www.springhole.net/writing_roleplaying_randomators/paranormal-and-weird-events.htm

⇨ http://www.springhole.net/writing_roleplaying_randomators/plot-punter_romance.htm

⇨ https://www.pinterest.ca/pin/179440366381817034/

Endnotes

1. Hill, Napoleon. "Belief." Napoleon Hill Foundation, October 5th, 2017, http://www.naphill.org/tftd/thought_for_the_day_thursday_october_5_2017/. Accessed: Jan. 03, 2018.

2. Robbins, Anthony. Money: Master the Game, Kindle Edition. Simon & Schuster 2014. Location: 788.7

3. Murray, Jacqui. "Word Count by Genre." Jacqui Murray's WordDreams Blog, December 8, 2010, https://worddreams.wordpress.com/2010/12/08/word-count-by-genre/. Accessed: Jan. 03, 2018.

4. Sambuchino, Chuck. "Word Count for Novels and Children's Books: The Definitive Post." WritersDigest.com, October 24, 2012, http://www.writersdigest.com/editor-blogs/guide-to-literary-agents/word-count-for-novels-and-childrens-books-the-definitive-post. Accessed: Jan. 03, 2018.

5. Blue. "Great Novels and Word Count." Indefeasible.WordPress.com, May 3, 2008, https://indefeasible.wordpress.com/2008/05/03/great-novels-and-word-count/. Accessed: Jan. 16, 2018.

6. Julius Caesar ? Act 1, Scene 2, Page 6, http://nfs.sparknotes.com/juliuscaesar/page_18.html

7. Kenower, William. "A Writer's Worst Fear." JaneFriedman.com, May 15, 2017, https://www.janefriedman.com/writers-worst-fear/. Accessed: Jan. 04, 2018.

8. Louise. "Track your time: find more time to write." SmallStepsGuide.co.uk, April, 2017, http://www.smallstepsguide.co.uk/track-your-time/. Accessed: Jan. 05, 2018.

9. Baty, Chris. "No Plot? No Problem!: A Low-Stress, High-Velocity Guide to Writing a Novel in 30 Days." Chris Baty, September 9, 2004, https://www.amazon.com/dp/0811845052. Accessed: Jan. 18, 2018.

10. Matthews, Dr. Gail. "Study demonstrates that writing goals enhances goal achievement." Dominican University of California, Jan. 5, 2017, https://www.dominican.edu/dominicannews/study-demonstrates-that-writing-goals-enhances-goal-achievement. Accessed: Jan. 18, 2018.

www.ingramcontent.com/pod-product-compliance
Lightning Source LLC
Chambersburg PA
CBHW070858050426
42453CB00012B/2254